Expressions of His Glory

12 Faith-Filled Women
—— Share ——
12 Hope-Filled Stories

Divine Works Publishing, LLC. Royal Palm Beach, Florida U.S.A

© 2023 Divine Works Publishing
Expressions of His Glory

All rights reserved. No part of this publication may be reproduced, stored in a retrieval system, or transmitted in any form or by any means, electronic, mechanical, photocopying, recording or otherwise without the prior permission of the publisher or in accordance with the provisions of the Copyright, Designs, and Patents Act 1988 or under the terms of any license permitting limited copying issued by the Copyright Licensing Agency.

The views expressed in this work are solely those of the author and do not necessarily reflect the views of the publisher, the publisher hereby disclaims any responsibility for them.

ISBN-13: 978-1-949105-57-5 (paperback)
ISBN-13: 978-1-949105-60-5 (eBook)

First Edition Published: 10/10/2023
Printed in the United States

Published by:
Divine Works Publishing
Royal Palm Beach, Florida USA
561-990-BOOK (2665)

www.DivineWorksPublishing.com

Dedication

This book is dedicated to a remarkable woman who endured numerous hardships. She grew up on a plantation in South Carolina, witnessing and experiencing many traumatic events during the times of slavery and poverty. Despite all the challenges, she met the love of her life at a young age, got married, and had a total of seven children (two transitioned as infants). In search of a better life for their family, they moved to South Florida where she obtained her GED and nursing certificate. She dedicated her life to the well-being of her husband, children, grandchildren, and everyone she loved or crossed paths with.

Unbeknownst to her, South Florida had many trials and tribulations awaiting. She faced cruelty and underhanded rejection from others in her community, including times when her own family treated her poorly. She experienced mental and emotional battles with all five of her living children, as they struggled with addiction, unhealthy relationships, and incarceration. She faced several embarrassing moments as others whispered rumors about her family.

This extraordinary woman crossed paths with at least nine out of the twelve women in this book and has touched their lives with her own story in a tremendous way. To many she was known as Hattie or Mrs. Cooper, but to me, she was my grandmother, my Mama. As her granddaughter, I can testify she was a woman who encountered the glory of God over and over again.

My grandmother had a special way of encouraging her children and grandchildren through heartfelt notes. It is my prayer that every story in this book will bring encouragement to others just as she intended with her own words of encouragement.

Missing Grandma today and always,
Your Granddaughter Tamika Baldwin

Contents

Story 1 | *No Greater Love* 1

Story 2 | *Insured by God* 5

Story 3 | *According to His Master Plan* 9

Story 4 | *Speaking the Word of God Over Your Life* 15

Story 5 | *From My Zombie Life to My Abundant Life* 19

Story 6 | *Every Victory Has a Back Story* 25

Story 7 | *His Glory Revealed* 29

Story 8 | *When God Shows Up* 35

Story 9 | *God is Close to the Brokenhearted* 41

Story 10 | *God's Promises Never Fail* 45

Story 11 | *No Body Told Me the Road Would be Easy* 49

Story 12 | *Evidence of Divine Glory* 55

Welcome to a journey illuminated by the divine light of faith and the transformative power of God's glory. In the pages that follow, you will encounter stories that echo the timeless truth found in Revelations 12:1, *"And they overcame him by the blood of the Lamb, and by the word of their testimony; and they loved not their lives unto death."* This sacred scripture has been our guiding star, compelling us to share the profound evidence of God's glory in our lives.

In this book, you will discover a collection of narratives that go beyond mere words – they are testament to the extraordinary grace that has shaped our existence. Each story is adorned with carefully curated *"quotables"* and **#hashtags**, not just to capture the essence of our experiences, but to invite you, dear reader, into a conversation. We believe that engagement, be it through social media or introspective thoughts, creates a tapestry of shared faith and solidarity among believers.

But this book is more than just a monologue; it is an invitation, a call to action. As you immerse yourself in these tales of triumph and divine intervention, we urge you to embrace the quotables, adopt the hashtags, and, most importantly, share your own testimony. Your voice is a beacon of hope, a ripple in the vast ocean of faith, and it deserves to be heard.

More than ink on paper, this book is a vessel designed to carry the *Expressions of God's Glory* to every corner of the world. It is a manifesto of positivity, a testament to the unwavering faith that resides within us all. As you embark on this journey, may you be inspired to spread the light, to share your story, and to encourage others through their trials.

Together, let us weave a narrative of faith, hope, and love, celebrating the boundless glory of the Almighty. Let us illuminate the world with our shared experiences, and in doing so, let us create a legacy of faith-filled content that echoes through generations.

And they overcame him by the blood of the Lamb, and by the word of their testimony; and they loved not their lives unto death.

#ExpressionsofHisGlory #ShareYourTestimony

1 | No Greater Love

No one has greater love [nor stronger commitment] than to lay down his own life for his friends. You are my friends if you keep on doing what I command you. I do not call you servants any longer, for the servant does not know what his master is doing; but I have called you [My] friends, because I have revealed to you everything that I have heard from My Father. (John 15:13-15)

Throughout my life, one of the biggest things God has delivered me from and is still working on is myself. My biggest issue being my mindset—which often felt dark and lacking clarity. Even back in elementary school, I recall constantly feeling discouraged and confused while others seemed to grasp things more easily. I unsuspectingly carried this negative mindset into my adulthood. By the time I was 17 and had my first child, people would tell me, "*Your life is ruined.*" And sadly, I believed them.

This type of thinking led me to not respect myself and engage in a toxic relationship. I felt trapped in my bad decisions, which eventually led to drug abuse and the removal of my children. However, it was during my lowest point that my perception began to change. God began revealing Himself to me, although I felt that I had done some terrible things. He showed up for me through random acts of kindness from strangers. It was in this place that God began to work on my hardened heart.

One example of the love God showed me occurred when I attended parenting classes to regain custody of my children. There was a man I met in the class with whom I would engage in small talk. One day, he noticed that I had gone a whole day without eating or drinking and didn't have any food or money. He offered me his food stamp card so I could have a meal. Later, I found out that this man was homeless. I learned valuable life lessons from him, including the importance of perception.

Although I often struggled to find my way, God continued pursuing me. During the process of regaining custody of my children, God showed me immense mercy. At the time, it felt incredibly challenging, but looking back it wasn't as difficult as it could have been. My children and I were granted much favor and I now realize it was all because of God's great love. I regained custody of my children a year and a half later. We have experienced both highs and lows, but we have overcome them all together. Even at this present moment in my life, God remains steadfast.

Twelve years later, His love continues to pursue me and change my heart. During my most difficult moments God has shown me that NO GREATER LOVE exists. His agape love has changed my mind and transformed my soul. My negative mindset has been completely overhauled because of God's great love.

I have moved to a new state and He has continuously used different people to show me how much He loves me. *"Surely, your goodness and mercy shall follow me all the days of my life."* (Psalms 23:6)

Truly, I have witnessed God's favor in my life. He has remained faithful to His word. I am grateful to God for gifting me this opportunity to share how I have experienced His great love.

As it is written in the scriptures, *"Not that I have already obtained all this, or have already reached my goal, but I press on to take hold of that for which Christ Jesus took hold of me"* (Philippians 3:12).

In my closing, no matter the low place you may find yourself in rest assure God's great love will see you through.

During my most difficult moments God has shown me that No Greater Love exists. His agape love has changed my mind and transformed my soul.

#NoGreaterLove #ExpressionsofHisGlory

Letitia Ponder

Letitia Ponder was Born and raised in Pompano Beach Florida, where she resided for 41 years. She was born to Evelyn Sutton and Willie C Ponder. She is the mother of 5 children Articia(24), Amirie(21), Jonathan (20), Ariel (17) and Ayden (14). In a leap of faith she and 4 of her 5 children moved to Lacey, Washington for a fresh start. Now with the help of God they are growing and thriving and enjoying God's blessings. She hopes and prays that her story helps someone see just how much our Heavenly Father is in love with them.

2 | *Insured by God*

A new chapter began in my life, where everything changed. At the age of 23 with a minimal education and five children from different fathers, I faced numerous challenges. By the time I turned 21, I experienced a mental breakdown and was diagnosed with Clinical Depression. Shortly after, I lost my beloved mother, this made everything even more difficult.

I was surrounded by odds that seemed stacked against me. Where I come from, it was common for others to label and stereotype someone like me. People considered us just another statistic. However, I'm grateful that their thoughts and words didn't determine our destiny. Instead, a divine presence entered my life, the insurance agent named Jesus, offering me a policy worth embracing.

During my darkest moments, when hope seemed like a forbidden word and the future appeared bleak; encompassed by trouble, pain and heartache, I contemplated suicide as the only way out. But my insurance agent, Jesus, saw things differently. It has been 29 years since I was presented with an insurance policy, comprising 66 books filled with precious promises guaranteeing life. Jesus Christ was the only one capable and equipped to introduce me to the ultimate CEO, God the Father, the insurer of us all.

I am immensely grateful to say that Jesus loved me despite my faults and my past life of ignorance. He didn't hesitate to insure me and my children by granting us a lifetime policy, as long as we abide by the agreement. This policy, called eternal life, covers all my past sins. The legal terms of this policy allow me to access healing benefits in four crucial areas: mentally, emotionally, physically, and spiritually. My five children have all grown into successful adults and I am privileged to witness the fulfillment of Jesus' promises in their lives as well.

Furthermore, Jesus has opened doors for me that I couldn't have imagined. From starting as a mere customer file prepper, I now serve as the department head of a company. I have also been blessed with beautiful grandchildren, a second generation of God's blessings. But above all I live a life filled with hope and anticipation.

The insurance plan provided by Jesus remains unchanged and guaranteed, sealed by His blood. I have availed myself of the bonus benefits ever since I enrolled in this policy. Just as other insurance agents offer free roadside assistance, Jesus has been my roadside assistance throughout the past 29 years. He has guided me and my family on this journey called life.

Therefore, I want to encourage anyone who finds themselves uninsured today to sign up now. The agent is waiting at the door, knocking on your heart. Please, by all means necessary, answer Him. The CEO (God), insurer of this policy, will never fail you. He will never leave you. He will never nor forsake you. He will love you unconditionally, regardless of your faults, mistakes, hurts or current situation. No matter what comes your way, He is more than willing to release His benefits for you.

Rest assured that on this journey called life, you will be covered. All you need to do is sign up for His policy. How can you sign up, you ask? It's simple and practical – just repeat after me: "Lord Jesus, I am in need of this policy today. I invite you to come into my life and insure me. I understand the need to confess with my mouth that you are Lord and believe in my heart that you were raised from the dead on the third day, possessing all power in your hands." If you sincerely say this from your heart, you are now saved and insured. Welcome to the family of God.

Take the time to read your policy book, the B.I.B.L.E, and find a faith-based church that preaches the true word of God. Allow Him to be God in your life from this day forward. Be assured, you will not be disappointed. I am a living witness, a satisfied customer of His, who takes great pleasure in sharing and spreading the good news of my lifetime policy.

To God be the glory for my life and for your life, now and forevermore. In Jesus' name, Amen.

The insurance plan provided by Jesus remains unchanged and guaranteed, sealed by His blood. I have availed myself of the bonus benefits ever since I enrolled in this policy.

#InsuredbyGod #ExpressionsofHisGlory

Starr Petty

Starr Petty is a wife and a mother of five successful adult children. She is also a proud grandmother of nine blessed grandchildren. She is a born again believer, a minister of the Gospel of Jesus Christ and has served in leadership positions at The Biblical House of God Church for over 29 years. Currently, she serves as a department head for DSN, an auto and tag company. Her deepest desire is to dwell in the house of the Lord forever and ever.

3 | According to His Master Plan

There is no way to predict the future. No one on this earth knows what lies ahead, not even you. You may consult a seer, psychic, prophet, or palm reader. You can analyze your horoscope, observe the moon, stars, clouds, or waves, yet still remain uncertain about your future. The only being aware of your next move is the Holy Divine One. The one who can account for your tears, steps, breaths in and out is Jesus. I had absolutely no way of knowing that within twelve months, there would be a significant turning point that would forever change my life. I will share this experience with you shortly.

I was born and raised in a devoutly religious household. During the development of my life while I was in my mother's womb, she experienced a spiritual awakening and developed a deep love and devotion for Christ. As a toddler, I spent a considerable amount of time with my siblings under my mother's care, while my father worked to support our family. Our lives revolved around our faith, guided by the Holy Spirit, and everything we did was aimed at glorifying God. Our daily routine consisted of beginning and ending our days with prayer. Growing up, we were not permitted to engage in secular activities such as dancing to non-religious music or wearing pants. Our commitment to our Christian values was evident in our regular attendance at church, despite its distance from our home. My mother truly exemplified dedication to God's calling.

It was during a church service at the age of twelve, while listening to my pastor, the late Elder Daniel E. Gainey, that I felt a strong desire to cultivate my own personal relationship with the Lord. My mind started racing with thoughts of relying on God throughout my life's journey - graduating high school, attending college, getting married, becoming a parent, retiring, and everything in between. I pondered the question, "Who would pray for me as I navigate this path?" Still seated in church, I began to earnestly plead with God to enter my heart. I expressed my need for His presence and guidance. I acknowledged my inability to make decisions alone and my uncertainty about which direction to take in life. With all sincerity, I implored Jesus, "I don't want to journey through this life without you. I need your help. Please stay by my side and support me. I am reliant on you, Jesus." Though my prayer lacked eloquence or flowery language, it originated from the depths of my soul. This marked the beginning of my personal relationship with God.

It didn't take me long to personally discover the ways of God. I would diligently read the Bible and my Sunday school book, seizing every opportunity to sing praises to God. I cherished my private moments of prayer and even took to writing down my heartfelt petitions. This newfound relationship with God guided me through my formative years, urging me to keep my mind, body, soul, and spirit pure, eagerly awaiting the arrival of Christ. Yes, I eagerly anticipated the rapture, the glorious return of our Savior. During those days, I was taught the importance of preparation, for Jesus could come at any moment. As a result, I quickly forgave others and regularly repented, valuing the precious connection I shared with Christ. I did everything in my power to ensure that my relationship with God remained untainted. I willingly attended church, devoting my time to teaching young children stories from the Bible, singing, playing the tambourine, participating in stage plays and dancing. My life served as a testament to the love in my heart for the Lord. Despite my deep connection with the Father, I remained unaware of the trials that lay ahead in my future. Never could I have imagined that my relationship with God was preparing me for something devastating, something that would shake my soul and challenge the very core of my being.

I was born and raised in a different state from my grandparents. However, in my thirties, a wonderful opportunity arose to live less than an hour away from them. Over the course of six years, I cherished every moment spent with them, often visiting and even spending long weekends in their company. The time I shared with them was an invaluable gift that I will forever treasure. We would engage in heartfelt conversations for hours. In addition to imparting a wealth of life lessons, my grandfather regaled me with stories of our family's history. Despite only having a grade school education, he possessed uncommon strength and wisdom. He was a skilled problem solver and his intelligence commanded respect within our family, among his peers, and within the community. My grandmother, on the other hand, radiated strength, sassiness, and a fierce determination. She possessed the rare combination of strength and gentle humility. Her sharp wit far surpassed her time, and she was a true trailblazer who ardently loved the Lord. One of the greatest gifts she bestowed upon me was teaching me the qualities of being a loving and devoted wife, and how to wholeheartedly love God.

I returned to my home state and shortly after, turmoil began. While working on a job I didn't love, I received a call from a family member asking me to come to the hospital. My father was about to undergo major surgery in less than 24 hours. At that moment, I realized that I hadn't spoken to my father in almost two years, as he had cut me off from his life. Within those two years, he had missed out on so much in my life, including the fact that I had moved back home. I was hesitant about going to the hospital, but I wanted him to know that I would be there for him despite our past. I arrived at the hospital and had a long and productive talk with my dad. I assured him that I would be by his side throughout his journey and we even prayed together.

The passing of my grandfather devastated me. He represented my past, present, and future. After his passing, I started having dreams of being lost in a dark place with no way out. It was an honor to sing at his funeral, as I stood on the podium trying to give comfort to my grandfather's friends and family. I remembered the strength of his legacy, the history of our family, and the path he paved so that I could strive for a better life and love people more deeply. Ten months later, my father also passed away, which left me completely shattered. I was seven months pregnant and felt utterly vulnerable. The absence of my father pushed me into immediate depression, where I lost my appetite and couldn't sleep. It put my unborn child at risk, and I found myself just going through the motions of work and home life. One day, I woke up in a pool of blood, fearing that I was losing the baby. In that moment of despair, I questioned God's presence in my life. But then, I had flashbacks of praying with my mother and grandmother, and I recalled the many joyful memories with my dad. I remembered how he would playfully mess up my hair or makeup when we greeted each other with a hug. I realized that he had always been there for me during my lowest moments. I also remembered the countless wise conversations I had with my grandfather, where he imparted advice that I didn't realize I would need in the future. Both of these influential men, who I always looked to for guidance, wisdom, and support, were no longer with me. They both left me within the same year, and I felt completely exposed and hopeless. But through all this pain, I understood that only God truly knows my future. He is the one who prepared me to handle the trauma of losing these important figures in my life. When I felt fatherless and alone, God was there. He is the one who sees my tears and understands my heart. He is the only one who truly knows me from within.

The men in my life were far from perfect, and I was aware of their flaws and imperfections. However, the wisdom, respect, honor, and knowledge they showcased were priceless. I see the strength of my father and grandfather reflected in my son every day. He is a direct heir to the strong men in my life. The Bible says, "A good man leaves an inheritance for his children's children." My son never had the chance to meet my father and grandfather, but through God's grace and mercy, we have been given the opportunity to carry their legacy and fulfill our own unique calling and destiny.

No one on this earth understands my needs and knows me like my heavenly father does. Jesus fulfills the role of a father in my life at times when I feel fatherless. He is a protector when I feel exposed and a sustainer when I'm broken. He places everything in my life according to His divine master plan. God truly is everything to me.

When I felt fatherless and alone, God was there. He is the one who sees my tears and understands my heart. He is the only one who truly knows me from within.

#AccordingtoHisMasterPlan #ExpressionsofHisGlory

Docia Metts

Docia Metts was born in South Florida in the 1970s to Joseph Metts Sr. and Delores (White) Metts. She has two siblings - one older brother (Joseph) and one younger sister (Angela). She graduated from Deerfield Beach High School, and attended Broward College in Coconut Creek, Florida, and later attended South Carolina State University in Orangeburg, South Carolina. She was a member of Church of God by Faith Inc. in Delray Beach, Florida, and later joined and diligently served at the Meeting Place Church of Greater Columbia, South Carolina. Docia has over 15 years of experience in the Finance industry, she currently resides in South Florida. She is a proud mother to one incredible child and an aunt to three beautiful children. Additionally, she is recognized as a mentor, business owner, intercessor, teacher and above all a daughter of the most high, King Jesus.

4 | Speaking the Word of God Over Your Life

My hope is that those who read my personal testimony will be inspired to speak God's word over any need or situation in their lives. By doing so, we invite God to work in a remarkable manner. Trust me, He will manifest His presence and work wonders! Unexpected life events have a tendency to sneak up on us. Even when we are doing everything right, something can happen out of the blue, completely altering the path of our lives. If you can relate to this, please know that you are not alone.

While I was on my way to work, a truck drove through the red light and collided with me head-on. The accident occurred so suddenly that I had no time to react defensively. It left me devastated and in excruciating pain, but at the same time, grateful to be alive. I realized that if it weren't for the grace of God, I would have lost my life.

The paramedics arrived promptly and transported me to the hospital. I was admitted and remained there for a week. The doctor diagnosed me with a fractured knee, which required a cast for support. However, three weeks after being discharged, my knee started swelling and the pain became unbearable. Concerned, I returned to the hospital, thinking I had overexerted myself and re-injured it.

In the emergency room, the doctor conducted tests and ordered X-rays. I wasn't prepared for the emotional blow his diagnosis delivered. He informed me that I had a blood clot, and there was a strong possibility it could travel to my heart. The hardest part to swallow was when he revealed that I had an 80% chance of dying. Despite feeling despair, fear, and questioning "Why me?" I eventually accepted reality and realized I needed to fight for my life.

To strengthen my resolve, I immersed myself in the word of God, listening to scripture on old cassettes. I played healing scriptures as I went to sleep and throughout the day. When I wasn't listening, I tuned in to the Christian Broadcast. Some may have seen these actions as radical, but I knew I needed to nourish my faith and gain strength to face this battle.

Please remember that in life, storms sometimes precede the calm periods. I spent over a month in the hospital, enduring the presence of monitoring devices, IVs, blood thinners, and numerous medications. Sadly, none of them seemed to effectively dissolve the blood clot. The doctor had warned that chest pain would indicate the clot had reached my heart. Yet, despite these circumstances, I persisted in speaking God's word.

These were the main scriptures which brought me comfort throughout this ordeal:

- *Psalm 118:17:* "I will not die, but I will live and proclaim what the Lord has done."

- Psalm 34:19: "Many are the afflictions of the righteous, but the Lord delivers him out of them all."

- Jeremiah 30:17: "For I will restore you to health and heal you of your wounds," declares the Lord.

- Jeremiah 33:3: "Call to me, and I will answer and show you great and mighty things, which you do not know."

- James 5:15: "And the prayer of faith will save the one who is sick, and the Lord will raise him up."

Even with these assurances, the blood clot still managed to reach my heart. As I lay in my hospital bed, the pain became unbearable, causing me to clutch the nearby curtain. It felt as if a tremendous weight had been placed on my chest, accompanied by sweating and difficulty breathing. Suddenly, I found myself falling from the bed to the floor.

Instinctively, I began reciting the latter part of Isaiah 53:5, "By His stripes, I am healed," repeatedly. Perhaps I uttered those words a hundred times before something remarkable occurred. That "something" was my healing! By the time the nurse and doctor entered my room, all the pain had vanished. God had miraculously restored my body and spared my life. Yes, by His stripes, I am healed. The doctor confirmed there were no blood clots and discharged me the following day. To God be the glory! The medical staff, who may not have been aware of God's healing power, witnessed it firsthand that day.

Whatever your need may be, speak God's word over it. His word offers wisdom, life, joy, peace, victory, prosperity, and healing. Search the scriptures, find the verses that address your specific situation, meditate on them, and speak them aloud. Remember, Proverbs 18:21 states, "Death and life are in the power of the tongue."

Do not give up! Place your complete trust in God. He may bring about a swift resolution to your situation, or He may allow you to endure for a while before intervening. Rest assured, He has neither forgotten nor abandoned you, so remain steadfast.

Understand that the word of God is one of the most powerful weapons at the disposal of a child of God. Live by it, speak it, apply it, and share it. May God bless you abundantly!

Instinctively, I began reciting the latter part of Isaiah 53:5, "By His stripes, I am healed," repeatedly. Perhaps I uttered those words a hundred times before something remarkable occurred. That "something" was my healing!

#SpeakingtheWordofGod #ExpressionsofHisGlory

Linda Carter

Linda Carter is a native of Milan, Georgia. She is the 6th child of 10 siblings. She is the loving mother of her one beautiful daughter, Melissa Carter Josey. Linda devoted over 30 years of her life to the medical field as a Nurses Assistant—leaving a lasting impression on patients, coworkers, and all whom she interacted with. Her charisma, loving spirit, dedication, and passion for what she did opened up many doors for her to be honored and recognized. Linda is truly a woman of God. She loves the Lord with all her heart, soul, mind, and strength. She has served in her local church congregation as a prayer warrior, choir member, and one who shares the word of God. Linda always encourages others with God's word, and acknowledges God as being the source of her strength. She indeed is an example of a believer and the epitome of grace.

5 | From Living My Zombie Life to Living My Abundant Life

In 2006, I found myself freshly divorced. I entered the den where my children were engrossed in watching "The Walking Dead." I couldn't help but wonder what kind of show it was. So, I decided to join them and watch a few episodes. As I watched, I saw myself - yes, it was as if I was living a zombie-like existence.

After 24 years of marriage, my husband and I decided to part ways. I became a true zombie, just like in "The Walking Dead." I was physically alive, but emotionally dead. I moved through my days without truly being present in my mind.

Allow me to explain further. Every day, I would wake up at 5 am, get my children ready, take them to school, come back home, clean, prepare dinner, get dressed, and head to work by 8:30 am. I worked until 6:30 pm or even later. During my one-hour lunch break, I would rush home to start cooking, scrambling to find a moment to eat while preparing the meal. I knew that once I finished work, I had to attend each child's school activities. One child was in middle school, while the other two were in high school.

Once we returned home, it became my responsibility to ensure everyone ate, completed their homework, and went to bed. Once everyone was asleep, I would get into my vehicle and drive to the beach, usually until 1 or 2 am. Then, I would return home and sleep for a mere two hours before starting the entire routine all over again. I continued this exhausting pattern for about four months. Yes, I was indeed living a zombie-like existence.

During this time, my mind was truly lost. I couldn't think for myself. I would simply smile when around others, all the while internally crying and blaming myself. I had no idea where my money was going; it seemed to vanish into thin air. I just couldn't seem to pull myself back together.

One night, as I found myself aimlessly walking on the beach, I thought to myself that if I continued walking towards the water, no one would miss me. I couldn't bear to live this way anymore; it felt as if my life was over.

Just as I made up my mind to take that fateful step towards the water, my phone rang. It was around 1 am. To my surprise, it was one of my old friends—someone I hadn't spoken to in a long time. I felt compelled to answer because something must have been wrong.

But when I answered, she seemed to be in a good mood. I could feel her smiling at me. Then she asked, "Where are you?" I was confused and replied, *"Huh?"* She repeated, "Where are you?" So, reluctantly, I answered her (I didn't want to tell her I was on the beach, walking toward the water to end it all). I turned around and headed back to the sidewalk, saying, *"I'm walking on the beach."*

As she continued talking, she asked, "Have you made it to your truck?" I replied, *"No."* She then said, "Go get in your truck. I'm going to talk to you until you get in your house." Following her instructions, I went to my truck and came home. I let her know I was in the house, said goodnight, and told her I loved her. I got into bed and fell asleep. She never knew she saved my life that night. God had sent her to be my savior. I recounted her the story 14 years later, how God used her to save me.

After that night, I stopped going to the beach, but I continued living a zombie-like life. One morning, I started experiencing chest pain, but I didn't say anything to my kids. I took them to school, came back home, and the pain intensified. One of my friends, who works at a cardiology office, called me. I told her what was happening, and she informed one of the nurses at her office. They urged me to come in immediately. They ran tests and determined that I was under a lot of stress, prescribing bed rest for a couple of weeks.

While I was at home, lying in bed, my phone rang. It was a realtor looking for my oldest daughter. I informed her that she was not there, and she began talking to me. I wasn't in the market to sell or rent, but a small voice inside me whispered, "Ask her what she has available for you to see." I followed that instinct and made an appointment with her. I picked up my youngest daughter from school and met with the realtor. She showed us various apartment complexes, but I wasn't pleased with any of them. I kept questioning myself why I was wasting this lady's time when I had no intention to move. However, she understood that I wanted to remain in the same area but then suggested an apartment that she thought I would genuinely like. It was located in a different city, which concerned me in terms of proximity to my job and my daughter's school.

When we arrived at the apartment, it was on the first floor. We went inside, and as I stepped into the living room, the sunlight flooded the space, and I instantly felt a sense of peace. It was as if the

Holy Spirit had entered the room, resting upon me. The Holy Spirit conveyed to me that this was where I needed to be. I inquired about the cost, and the realtor mentioned that similar apartments typically rented for $1400 and up. However, for that particular unit, they were only asking for $1100, and they required only the first month's rent.

It was clear to me that in order to rid myself of toxicity, I needed a change. And so, God heard my prayers and made it happen. I sold my house and moved.

During those years, I knew something needed to change, but I wasn't sure what or how. I relied on Psalm 27 and Psalm 37 for guidance. I also began seeing a therapist. Once my daughter graduated and went to college, I still felt a void, a longing for something more. That's when my best friend and I decided to move in together. I was finally stepping into a life of peace.

Two years later, I was diagnosed with breast cancer. I was devastated, and my mind felt clouded with despair. I wondered if I would ever see my family and friends again. I questioned how this could happen when I consistently went for annual exams. Was it hereditary? I learned that my mother had breast cancer ten years ago but never shared that information with me. I decided to take the BRCA test to ensure my daughters wouldn't have to go through this ordeal.

I am grateful for my support system. They have been the best I could ask for. My mother, my children, my grandkids, my youngest brother and his wife, and my best friends stood by my side throughout the surgeries and treatments I had to endure. As I went through the treatments, I had ample time to reflect and realize the root cause of this disease. God was able to speak to me, and I was willing to listen.

One evening, my third daughter was staying with me during my healing period, and she became scared when she felt something on her breast. I advised her to call her father, who was supposed to have insurance for the kids until they turned 25. However, he had canceled the insurance. As we argued back and forth about why he would do this, he said something that deeply hurt me. He said, "I hope you die of cancer," knowing well that I was going through treatments. I was furious and retaliated by telling him that the grave he was digging for me, he should also dig two more, one for himself and his wife.

But God spoke to me and told me that although He could heal the disease, I needed to forgive. I had been carrying hate within me for years, not realizing the damage I was causing myself. Throughout my life, I harbored all the mental and physical abuse, along with the discrimination I faced because of the color of my skin. I had built a shield of hate to protect my heart, and this shield had become a part of me.

Most of the hate came from people close to me: my grandmother, father, mother, aunts, uncles, ex-husband, ex-mother-in-law, and my oldest daughter's father. Each of them played a role in breaking my heart into countless pieces and transforming it into a ball of hate. I accumulated so much hate inside me that I needed to release it, or else it would consume me, not the disease.

First, I had to forgive myself for hating each one of them. Then, I forgave them for their actions, allowing all that hate to be released, empowering me to move forward with my life. I began studying the concept of love, realizing that it is a commandment from God. I discovered that love was always within me, waiting to be released. After 50 years of searching, I finally understood that the key was to let love flow from within. Once I began to learn more about myself, I started to genuinely love.

Now, I can confidently say that I am no longer living a zombie-like existence, and I am cancer-free. Life has so much more to offer, and there are countless things I want to do and achieve because I have found love within myself.

I began studying the concept of love, realizing that it is a commandment from God. I discovered that love was always within me, waiting to be released.

#ZombieLifetoAbundantLife   #ExpressionsofHisGlory

Janit Mann Garner

Janit Mann Garner was born in Alma, GA in 1964. She is the proud mother of five adult children, including four daughters and one son. Additionally, she cherishes the joy of having ten grandchildren. Janit completed her education at Deerfield High School and pursued further learning by taking college courses at the University of Florida and Broward Community College.

Moreover, she dedicated an impressive 24 years of her life volunteering with the Deerfield Packer Rattler football and cheerleaders. Furthermore, Janit devoted three years of her time volunteering with the Deerfield Raiders football and cheerleaders. Janit's commitment to these organizations has awarded her a place on the alumni board for Deerfield Packer Rattler football and cheerleaders.

In her professional career, Janit worked diligently for the Broward School Board and the United States Postal Service. After serving many years, she retired from the United States Postal Service in 2018, at the age of 52. Nowadays, Janit finds joy in helping raise her grandkids. Janet has a strong belief in using the knowledge God has bestowed upon her to help others. Her motto is to *"help people by helping others with the knowledge God has given me"*.

6 | Every Victory Has a Back Story

Where do I begin? Every victory has a story. In May of 2006, I graduated from high school and faced the decision of which college to attend. I turned to God for guidance and felt a strong conviction in my heart to enroll at Nova Southeastern University. Both my aunt and cousin had successfully completed their degrees there, so I decided to follow in their footsteps.

However, God had other plans for my life. During my second year of college, I changed my major to Podiatry, aspiring to become a foot doctor. Unfortunately, in that same semester, I failed anatomy. Over the next few years, I changed my major multiple times, eventually settling on Accounting. Throughout this process, I sought the Lord's guidance, praying and fasting to discern my true career path. Alongside this search, my life took an unexpected turn. I transitioned from relying solely on my parents for financial support to helping them with their finances. This change was brought about by my father's need for brain surgery, a circumstance that left us uncertain of the outcome. During this challenging time, we placed our trust in the Lord, and I made the difficult decision to drop out of college and pursue a full-time job.

Though my heart was heavy with the desire to continue my education, I knew that my parents had sacrificed a great deal for me. I couldn't be selfish. So, I embraced my full-time job and persevered. It was during this period that my best friend, Brittany, obtained her master's degree. Her accomplishment served as an inspiration, urging me to consider returning to school.

Instead of returning to Nova, I enrolled at Broward College in 2015. My first semester, I took two classes. While I passed one, I unfortunately failed the other. Determined to complete my education, I persisted, taking one class per year until 2018. It was in that year that I made a decree and declaration to myself: I would take more than one class per year from then on. The journey from 2018 to 2022 was challenging, but with God's strength and guidance, I pressed forward, relentlessly pursuing my goals.

My final semester I contemplated giving up. However, thanks to the encouragement of my professor, Ms. Lopez, I found the motivation to keep going. She reminded me that God had brought me this far for a reason and encouraged me to finish the course with only three weeks remaining. As the time for graduation approached, I was filled with gratitude. I thanked the Lord for His faithfulness and as I walked across the stage, I continuously praised Him, declaring that all glory belonged to God.

The journey I have shared with you is a testament to the words of Jeremiah 29:11, which states, *"For I know the thoughts that I think toward you, saith the Lord, thoughts of peace, and not of evil, to* give you an expected end." Every victory comes with a story, and this is my story. I give all the glory to God, who made this possible for me. Through this experience, the glory of God has been revealed in my life, and I am forever grateful to my Lord and Savior.

She reminded me that God had brought me this far for a reason and encouraged me to finish the course with only three weeks remaining. As the time for graduation approached, I was filled with gratitude. I thanked the Lord for His faithfulness and as I walked across the stage, I continuously praised Him, declaring that all glory belonged to God.

#EveryVictoryHasaBackStory #ExpressionsofHisGlory

Melissa Carter Josey

Melissa Carter Josey, a Florida native, was raised in a home where both parents faithfully served the Lord with all their hearts. Melissa dedicated her life to the Lord at a young age, and her walk with Christ has continuously grown as she transitioned into adulthood. She is a devoted wife, daughter, and friend, and she has achieved an associate degree while actively pursuing her bachelor's degree in business. In all her encounters, Melissa shares the love of Christ. She remains committed to serving the Lord with all her heart, soul, mind, and strength, knowing that her labor is not in vain.

7 | His Glory Revealed

*"Jesus answered,
Neither hath this man sinned, nor his parents:
but that the works of God should be made manifest in him."
-John 9:3 (NKJV)*

Growing up as a child I was taught "you reap what you sow & do unto others as you would have them do unto you." These became words to live by. Although my mom was raised in the church we didn't attend church regularly. However, my mother ensured that my siblings and I were taught biblical principles and Sunday mornings were filled with gospel music on the radio. Sunday dinner was always a delightful feast.

Fast forward to my senior year of high school. I remember being fearful as a 16-year-old girl giving birth to a vibrant, bouncy baby boy. It was a Sunday morning on March 17th at 3:09 a.m. I remember reading the Bible to my baby, as I had read that babies can hear even in the womb. Little did I know that this moment would become a turning point in my life.

One warm summer day, my son was about 3 months old at the time. I was sitting on the front porch with my mother. I watched my mom cradle my son as his big beautiful eyes seemed to go into a daze. His chubby arms and legs began to jerk for about 10 seconds, which felt like an eternity at the time. After graduating from high school, instead of preparing for college and new jobs like my classmates, I embarked on a journey of taking my son to hospitals and doctors' offices. We spent a month in a local hospital with EEG leads attached to his thick black curly hair. My son was diagnosed with infantile spasms, and thus began our encounters with neurologists, lab work and seizure medications.

As I navigated through this challenging time, I began to ask God who or what I had done wrong. After all I misunderstood what my mother told me as a child. "What goes around comes back around." I was constantly crying, scared, confused, and broken, asking God "Why?" Although I knew of God, I was uncertain about how to pray for myself and my baby. Fortunately, my mother was a prayer warrior who interceded for us. And all the while, through the darkness, God was revealing His glory.

As we continued our visits to doctors and received diagnoses, I came to terms with the fact that my baby was not meeting developmental milestones. My aunt, my mother's sister, invited me to the church they were raised in. It was there, shortly after, that I gave my life to Christ. I started attending church regularly, still carrying questions and doubts in my heart, wondering why this thing that I perceived to be "*Bad*" was happening to me. But God continued to reveal His glory.

Soon after giving my life to Christ, we still faced seizures almost daily. My mother and I spent countless nights trying to console my crying baby. During one such night, I had a dream about my son and I. In the dream I was in a church service, and an unfamiliar woman approached me and began to pray, saying, "Lord, it's time." I began praising God, and I looked towards the altar, where I saw my son standing, whole and healed. Shortly before waking up, I heard a voice say, "Your child shall be dismissed." As I woke up, God led me to the book of Revelations and Chapter 12, which speaks of a woman who gave birth to a man child and how the enemy sought to destroy him. But God intervened and revealed His glory. I thought that because I was now saved and beginning to pray that my son would be healed instantly, but God was still revealing His glory.

In my brokenness and confusion, I turned to reading the Bible, even though I didn't fully comprehend everything I read. Many of us are taught that what happens in our lives (good or bad) is because of what we have done right or wrong. By God's guidance, I came across the scripture in John 9:3, which spoke directly to my heart and mind. As I read those words, it was as if I was looking into a mirror. It wasn't just what I believed people were saying about me, but also the thoughts and feelings I had about myself. The very thing that made people stare, whisper, and made me feel vulnerable and defensive was the very thing God had chosen to unveil and reveal His presence in my life.

Many divine situations are hidden treasures in these earthen vessels, handpicked by God. The very piece of Himself, He has deposited in us for the world to see His glory. However, we often try to camouflage, bury, or cover up these treasures because society teaches us to hide what we perceive as weaknesses. We may feel embarrassed or ashamed of things beyond our control. But these are the very things that reveal God's glory within us. I have learned that my complete dependence on God allows me to experience His glory most fully.

The glory of God is evidence of His presence, and He is most visible in our human weaknesses. Our limited vision may hinder us from seeing this truth. We may misunderstand why our good and great God allows us to experience immense pain and suffering. But it is through these trials that the weight of God's glory is revealed. The unveiling of God's presence is not for others to realize, but for us to see with our spiritual vision. It is in these moments that God manifests Himself most in our lives.

So, the very thing that initially made me wonder "why" now shows me how God entrusted me with carrying the weight of His glory on a level that I may have never known had I not given birth to his chosen vessel. My son has taught me more in his silence than I could ever teach him, even with a thousand words. I now understand the scripture that reads, *"God maketh wise the simple"* (Psalm 19:7 -KJV).

This journey of blood, sweat, and tears has taught me that it's not the things I desire to display as trophies to the world that reveal the glory of God within me. It is the things I would prefer to conceal that truly illuminate the reflection of His image in me. I never imagined that this tiny bundle of flesh and blood could contain the immeasurable and incomprehensible glory of our loving Father and Creator. Now, I can hold my head up high and raise my hands in praise, knowing that *"His strength is made perfect in my weakness"* (2 Corinthians 12:9 -KJV).

It's not the things I desire to display as trophies to the world that reveal the glory of God within me. It is the things I would prefer to conceal that truly illuminate the reflection of His image in me.

#HisGloryRevealed #ExpressionsofHisGlory

Shanette D. Cain

Shanette D. Cain is a 44-year-old mother to her one son, Tyrell R. Cain. She is the youngest of thirteen children and has always had the heart of a servant. The birth of her son caused her to realize a strong desire to help & care for people. In 2011, she graduated from Williamsburg Technical College in South Carolina. She received her license in practical nursing and continues to work in the medical field. Shanette's career as well as her relationship with GOD has afforded her many opportunities to share her testimony. She has been an adult Sunday school teacher for over 17 years. She remains a student to the word of God and enjoys decorating, spending time with her family, and meeting new people.

8 | When God Shows Up

There have been numerous occasions when God has shown up in my life. The first instance was when I believed in Him for a miracle regarding my health. I was born with an abnormal heart valve and was supposed to undergo open heart surgery at the age of 11. However, the surgery was postponed until I was 21, and I was informed that I could not have a natural childbirth.

At the age of 27, I welcomed the Lord into my life and placed my faith in Him after reading Hebrews 13:8, which states that, "Jesus Christ remains the same yesterday, today, and forever". I asked the Lord if He would still perform miracles today if we have the audacity to believe His word, and I decided to trust Him completely. I discarded all of my medications and whenever the chest pains became unbearable, I stood firmly on the word of God. He manifested His presence and after some time, the pain vanished. This experience solidified my belief that the word of God works effectively when we trust it, speak it, and obey it. Consequently, my faith began to soar.

God's intervention was evident once again during my third pregnancy. For my first two children, I had to rely on the expertise of specialists due to my previous medical conditions. However, since I had embraced faith in God, I decided to step out in faith for my third and fourth child by seeking care at a local clinic rather than at specialized facilities that I had previously visited. With unwavering conviction and trust in the word of God, I sought treatment at the clinic, and indeed, God showed up. I experienced a natural childbirth without any complications. What an awe-inspiring God we serve!

Several years later, God once again revealed His presence during my fourth child's birth. Although the small hospital connected to the clinic I used to visit had shut down, I had to go to a larger advanced hospital for the delivery. The doctors noticed my previous open-heart surgery and proceeded with additional tests immediately after the birth. Although they put me through a series of medical examinations, the results were inconclusive, and they recommended further testing. I knew deep in my heart that God had already made a miraculous restoration within my body. With conviction, I took my child and left the hospital, explaining that I trusted in God's healing power. My faith was put to the test once again, when I discovered that I owed the IRS thousands of dollars because of my estranged husband's unpaid taxes. I informed the IRS agent of our separation, and to my surprise, he separated our files and did not pursue any claims against me. Shortly thereafter, my husband passed away, and the IRS was unable to seize any of my assets or money. They further revealed that the employee who separated our files was no longer employed at the agency. God had intervened in my life long before I even became aware of it. Trusting in Him yields magnificent results. Amen!

During another challenging period my house was in foreclosure. A hurricane struck, causing a tree to fall on my home and the county authorities came to my aid and provided temporary shelter for my children and I. After a considerable period had passed, I realized that the house was no longer mine. However, upon the suggestion of my son, I decided to investigate further and discovered that my late husband obtained homeowner's insurance for the property. This unexpected turn of events allowed me to repair the house and sell it to the school board, which provided them with an opportunity to expand its facilities. God undeniably continued to show up for me and I am forever grateful for the favor He bestowed upon my life. Whenever His favor is present, He reveals Himself. God desires to bless us more than we desire to be blessed.

Permit me to express how God continues to show up repeatedly. I vividly recall the time when I applied for an apartment in a senior citizen building. I was informed that there was a lengthy waiting list and that some people had been waiting for two to three years. In response, I began to thank God for my new place to live, expressing my gratitude by speaking His word. Astonishingly, after just two months, I received a call to visit and view my potential apartment. God indeed showed up, and I did not have to endure a prolonged wait. I continued to express my thankfulness and praise to Him, as the song goes *"I Believe God"* so aptly states. Trust, obedience, and faith are essential in experiencing His divine presence. Amen!

Another instance of God's intervention occurred when I was involved in a severe car accident. The impact was akin to being hit by a train. The weather was inclement, and I was driving my daughter's vehicle cautiously due to heavy rain. Unfortunately, a young lady behind me was driving at an excessive speed despite the adverse weather conditions and collided into the back of my car. Although her car was completely totaled, my daughter's vehicle sustained minimal damage due to its size. Nonetheless, the magnitude of the impact affected my eardrums and eyes. When the police inquired about my well-being and whether I needed medical attention, I assured them that I was fine, fully aware of the routine medical procedures that would occur at the emergency room. Yet again, I recognized that God had consistently shown up in my life. This time, I had to reaffirm my trust in Him. He is the same God who had guided me when I discarded all my medications and experienced two natural childbirths. He is the same God who had intervened when the IRS confronted me. I never ceased to speak His word during these encounters, and I found myself again in a similar position, relying on His ongoing strength. My left ear and eyes were severely affected, yet I chose to remain silent about it to my children, confidently assuring them that I was alright. I continually declared Isaiah 53:5, which declares healing through Christ's wounds. My ears eventually recovered, but my eyes still experienced some difficulties. Nevertheless, I persisted in speaking God's word, and one day, my vision became perfectly clear. His word manifested in my ears and once more, He showed up!

I refrained from seeking formal eye examinations, trusting in God's miraculous ability to restore my vision. Eventually, I regained complete clarity and perception. When the time came to renew my driver's license, I contemplated exchanging it for a Florida ID since I no longer owned a vehicle and believed that it was unnecessary due to my advancing age. However, after reconsidering, I decided to renew it. I confidently underwent the vision test, reading the letters as perfectly as if I were in my thirties—despite being in my seventies—I do not require glasses.

Allow me to share another chapter of my faith journey: "When God Shows Up!" The Lord's intervention was especially meaningful during the COVID-19 pandemic. As someone in their seventies, I began experiencing symptoms throughout my body. The enemy whispered words of vulnerability due to my age group being the most prone to the virus. However, in the face of this attack, I firmly stood on the word of God. I declared Ephesians 6:10 and Galatians 3:13, affirming my strength in the Lord and His redemption from all curses. I refused to speak anything other than God's word, even when weakened physically. Instead, I proclaimed Joel 3:10, stating that the weak can declare strength. God showed up!

The fever subsided, and my strength returned. I attended to some essential matters, and wherever I went, temperature checks were mandatory. Yet, to my relief, my temperature always read normal. When we stand firm on God's word, it eventually comes to pass. This is His way of revealing Himself.

Furthermore, I had to combat the spirit of fear actively. So, I habitually made this confession: *"The love of God resides within me and surrounds me. God is love, and perfect love eradicates all fear from the enemy. I choose to walk in perfect love, in faith, through Jesus' mighty name. Fear has no place within me, according to 1 John 4:18."* Fully trusting and acting on God's word will surely result in His divine presence. To believe is to act. It requires acknowledging and confessing our past lack of trust in God and wholeheartedly seeking the assistance of His Holy Spirit.

We must exercise caution regarding our speech and the influence it imparts to the atmosphere, never underestimating the power of our words. Proverbs 18:21 reminds us that *"life and death are in the power of the tongue, and we shall eat the fruit thereof."* Our words possess life-changing power.

When we dare to trust and believe in Him, He invariably shows up. Amen!

Fully trusting and acting on God's word will surely result in His divine presence. To believe is to act.
#WhenGodShowsUp #ExpressionsofHisGlory

Dorothy Gregory

Dorothy Gregory is a mother of four children, twelve grandchildren and eleven great grandchildren. She is a minister who specializes in personal inner healing for the gospel of Jesus Christ. She is also a prayer warrior and a trailblazer for new converts to Christ. Dorothy also served as a chaplain for a women's state prison. In addition, she has devoted her time to community outreach ministries including jail, prison, and drug rehabilitation facilities. Dorothy trained men and women through workshops to equip them for various roles in outreach ministries. It is her heart's desire to see the entire body of Christ be healed and delivered through God's word.

9 | God is Close to the Brokenhearted

Writing my testimony, a place I have never been, caused a familiar darkness to envelop me. This darkness is what I am journeying through at this very moment. It is challenging to share from this dark place, but at the same time I am comforted to share my journey. I believe God designed me for this moment to help heal the broken, wounded, and lost souls. I have learned to embrace the dark times and find God's greater purpose guiding others to the loving embrace of the Lord.

He heals the brokenhearted and binds up their wounds.
Psalm 147:3

In times of deep sorrow, we often long for the comfort of loved ones, but when they are no longer with us, the pain can be devastating. I experienced the loss of my father, sister, and best friend; a series of tragedies that could have broken me. But through it all, I found solace in God's grace and the wisdom to humble myself before Him.

As I delved deeper into a personal relationship with Jesus, I learned to cast all my anxieties on Him, trusting that He cares for me. With God's plan active in my life, healing began to take place, transforming the hurt and brokenness into strength and purpose. God became my constant companion, even when my brave face hid the pain and weakness within.

Through my experiences, I realized the power of trusting in the Lord. He mended all my brokenness, fought my battles, and unveiled my true gifts. Knowing the Lord brought joy and love to my heart and gave me the strength to keep moving forward.

Reflecting on my past, I recognized that God's guidance led me from a life filled with rebellion to one of ministry. He turned my struggles into a legacy that I cherish. By surrendering my life to Christ, I found peace and redemption, allowing God to carry my burdens.

Prayer became a pillar of strength, as I witnessed the transformation in my life and the lives of others. Drawing on the strength of my Wonderwoman, my mother, I realized that God places strength in front of us for a reason, to uplift and empower us on our journey. Though the pain of loss is undeniable, I learned that God's reasons are not for us to understand but to trust in His glory. By embracing prayer and developing a strong prayer life, God's presence becomes evident in us. Our past struggles no longer define us, as we begin to glow with God's light.

In times of despair, it may feel like we are alone, but God is always by our side. As I faced the darkness of loss, God delivered me and renewed my purpose. I know my loved ones watch over me as angels, cheering me on to continue their legacy.

God's purpose for each of us is unique, and although we may not always comprehend it, trusting in the process allows His manifestation in our lives. Letting go and letting God guide our path brings transformation and glory.

So, as I continue this marathon of life, I find strength in the love and legacy of my family. God has delivered me, washed me over again, and I know my loved ones are proud of me. Their memory propels me forward, as I arise and shine in the glory of the Lord.

In conclusion, be encouraged to let go and let God lead your path. Trust the process, hold on to God's unchanging hand, and witness the manifestation of His glory in your life.

God's purpose for each of us is unique, and although we may not always comprehend it, trusting in the process allows His manifestation in our lives.

#GodisClosetotheBrokenHearted #ExpressionsofHisGlory

Merilyn Strowbridge

Merilyn Strowbridge is no ordinary woman, she is a role model to women and young girls. Strowbridge founded the organization Ambitious Queens; an organization which empowers and enhances females to grow in their self-confidence. The vision and mission of Ambitious Queen Organization is to encourage and empower women to know who they are and embrace that they are Royalty. She also hosts under the umbrella of Ambitious Queens an awareness of heart disease movement in honor of her sister, the late Gereldean Major, as well as One Hour of Strength Talk Show, topic: Life After Losing a Loved One.

10 | God's Promises Never Fail

Sometimes it feels like God's promises fail us and that He has forgotten about us. We may lose hope and wonder if there is anyone we can truly trust. But in Proverbs 3:5, we are reminded to trust in the Lord and not rely on our own understanding, no matter the circumstances. God's promises never fail.

Before we can experience God's glory, there is often a story of pain and suffering. My own story feels like a constant source of pain with experiences of separation, child neglect, and abusive relationships which included emotional and mental trauma. But God promised to mend my broken heart.

I grew up without knowing my father. I longed to see his face and understand who he was. It was a struggle, but in Jeremiah 1:5, it says that God knew me even before I was formed in the womb.

When I was twelve years old my mother became involved in an intimate relationship that caused her to prioritize fleshly pleasure over her responsibility as a mother. As a result, my brother and I were separated. My mother couldn't see the pain in our eyes nor hear our cries. During this time, I worried about my brother's well-being. As the days turned into months, I hoped for my mother to return, but she never did. My brother ended up homeless, while I became a maid, working for shelter and a small portion of food. The workload was overwhelming for a young child, but as written in Psalm 27:10, I held onto the promise that even when my parents forsake me, the Lord will take me up and teach me His ways.

One rainy night, in my weakness and desperation, I cried out to God for help not knowing how to pray. In that moment, God looked beyond my faults and saw my needs. He embraced me, and I felt His presence like I had never experienced before. In Jeremiah 31:13, He promised to turn our mourning into joy, to comfort us in our sorrow. That night, I made a covenant with God to serve Him no matter what.

From the age of twelve to eighteen, I moved through different foster care homes, refusing to allow any sexual abuse to overpower me. These transitions led me to isolate myself from society and struggle with mental health issues such as neglect, depression, suicidal thoughts, and low self-worth. But amidst these struggles, I held onto St. John 14:26, knowing that the Holy Spirit would be my helper, teaching and guiding me. God's glory will be revealed in me.

In 1989, God opened the door for me to migrate from Jamaica to the Bahamas. There, I worked as a caretaker for a wealthy family on Paradise Island. Just as Joseph was taken through trials in Genesis 37, God brought me from being homeless to a place called Paradise.

In 1993, I migrated to the United States where I met and married my husband. He has been a source of love, support, and provision. In 2 Corinthians 1:3-4, God promised to send me a comforter, and my husband has fulfilled that promise.

In 2022, I was diagnosed with stage 4 metastatic breast cancer, but by 2023, it went into remission. Ephesians 3:20 reminds us that God's power is at work in us, able to do infinitely more than we can ask or imagine. And as Isaiah 53:5 says, we are healed by His stripes. I will always hold onto His promises because they never fail. From birth until now God's promises have been revealed in my life. I will always hold steadfastly to God's promises. Allow me to encourage you to find the promises of God that meet your circumstances and hold on to them. I assure you He will never fail.

But amidst my struggles, I held onto St. John 14:26, knowing that the Holy Spirit would be my helper, teaching and guiding me.

#GodsPromisesNeverFail #ExpressionsofHisGlory

Juliet Cooper

Juliet Cooper was born on May 26th in the capital city of Kingston, Jamaica. She is the ninth child of ten siblings. She is a dedicated wife to her loving and hardworking husband, Bobby Cooper. Together they have three wonderful children: two daughters; Melissa and Vediesha, and a son Deiondre. Additionally, they have four grandchildren: three granddaughters; Keziah, Nevaeh, and Neriah and one grandson; Zachary. Her educational journey began at a basic school in Jamaica and she attended a primary high school. She received vocational training in childcare nursing, in eleventh and twelfth grade and completed her training at Jubilee Children's Hospital in Jamaica. Juliet migrated from Jamaica to Nassau, Bahamas where she pursued her degree in early childhood education. She then migrated from Nassau, Bahamas to the United States of America where she became a certified teacher in early childhood education for special needs at Broward Community College. At the age of twelve she accepted Christ into her life at Christ Temple Apostolic Church in Jamaica. She later joined Cathedral Church of God, where she served on the usher board for 20 years and eventually became an usher leader and taught children at church. Her mission for the kingdom of God is to become a missionary. Juliet's motto is, *"Only what is done for Christ will last,"* -2 Corinthians 4:18. Her mission for the kingdom of God is to become a missionary.

11 | No Body Told Me the Road Would Be Easy

Nobody told me the road would be easy and I don't believe He's brought me this far to leave me -Mary Mary

As I stepped into the dungeon of fire and darkness of substance abuse, my mind, soul, and will became enslaved to crack cocaine. It appeared I was on the road of no return and my grave eagerly awaited me. I relinquished my whole being and entered into the world of Latonya's real-life horror show.

With my spiritual grave clothes on I became a vessel for demonic spirits to freely enter and possess me. Lying, stealing, and cheating; feelings of embarrassment, shame, and suicidal thoughts became a part of my daily life. The devil thought he had me for life, BUT GOD had other plans for my life.

I grew up on the south side of Chicago in the notorious projects called "Robert Taylor" better known as the "Black Belt," where killing, stealing, drug abuse, gambling, gangsters and child predators were the norm. It was written and documented that the Robert Taylor projects were the worst place to live and that people who lived in the community would perish there and not make it out of the ghetto.

I had become a target statistic of this belief and was doomed to fail. My mother was a corporal punisher. She believed in whippings, beatings, extension cords, brooms, guns, and even an ax. That was her way of communicating. My mom was a single parent of seven children, 4 girls and 3 boys. We all adhered to her strict rules because we knew a beating ensued any disobedience.

We all had different fathers. I guess I can say my mother was a rolling stone. My dad was amazing, he always cared about my wellbeing and took care of me and I visited him often.

My mother had her own vices, like gambling and going to the racetrack. These habits led to us being evicted from the projects, but thankfully we were eventually allowed back in.

My uncle, Willie Jones, was the positive male figure in my life. He was an extraordinary uncle, daddy and father-figure to my family. He took care of us and brought joy to our household with his humor and countless acts of kindness. His jokes were funny as he would walk in the house and put the groceries on the table and proceed to pick all of us up one at a time and lightly throw us up in the air. Then after that he would go to the refrigerator, open the door and say "look at all this food in here" but in reality, there was no food. Then he would proceed to fill the refrigerator with all the goodies he brought.

During my wandering years as a teenager, I enjoyed a range of activities like dancing, sports, and exploring my entrepreneurial skills as a hair braider and ear piercer. However, I was also introduced to marijuana and alcohol at the age of thirteen. I had no idea that the portal of damnation had opened in my life. I was damming my life to a life of cataclysm, doom, and misfortune as I took the first plunge into experimenting with gateway drugs. At the time it seemed a fun and normal teen thing to do.

As I delved deeper into substance abuse, my behavior became more rebellious. I ran away, frequently clubbed, skipped school, and engaged in sex. I began comparing myself to other girls who appeared to be better than me. I also developed a complex within myself regarding my skin color, the way I talked, how skinny I was, and how I thought white people had it better than black folks. One of my major issues was I felt rejected by my mother and craved her love and acceptance. I tried so hard to please her. All I wanted to hear from her was "I Love You".

One day in 1981, at the age of sixteen I rebelled against my mom because I would not let her beat me. The next week I was on a plane to Texas where my oldest sister lived. I could not believe she sent me away with no hesitation. At this time in my life, I dropped out of school and started working at Church's Chicken with my sister. With no mother around I started being promiscuous.

Without any guidance or life skills, I struggled to navigate life on my own. I had no manual, no instructions, and no real-life skills. In most cases I was passive, shy, and in desperate need of being loved. My knowledge of Jesus was limited but still present.

In 1985, I had my first child, Deandra, at the age of 21. I lived on my own in government housing, collected food stamps and was unskilled. In 1986 I gave birth to my son Devone, and in 1987 my daughter, Denise came along; all of which had different daddies. It appeared I was following the footsteps of my mother.

I was still drinking and smoking until the man I was dating came home one day excited about smoking crack and he said to me, "You just gotta try it" and I did. For four years, my life became a living hell, and I lost everything. Life as I knew it was gloom and doom. The dark side of my life came upon me like a tsunami, an erupted volcano, and a hurricane all at once.

Within my four years of being a full-blown addict I hit rock bottom, became homeless, moved around from shelter to shelter and lived with other drug abusers.

Then the sun shined on me again when I moved to Austin, Texas and met my husband. At that time, we were both abstinent from drugs. During our eight years of marriage, I gave birth to two wonderful daughters Desiree and Dominique. Then my husband and I relapsed together and it was a horror show all over again. We found ourselves trapped, living in drug-infested places and hotels with our children. Life was so bad that we sold our food stamps and pawned any and all valuable items just to survive. Life was empty. During my last pregnancy, my daughter, Dominique was born crack addicted and the Department of Family Services took all my children away and placed them in a foster home. It was the worst day of my life.

In 1991, Jesus restored and recovered my life with His salvation. I became deeply involved in the church taking on various roles and responsibilities. I earned the title State Evangelist. I was ordained as a minister; I had a street ministry and a radio show. I walked in my calling and raised my children in the admiration of the Lord. I pursued higher education and earned my associate degree in early childhood education.

Amidst of my victories, tragedy struck my family in 2007 when my oldest daughter was brutally shot and killed. After the detectives left my home, I immediately fell on my knees and said, "Lord, I know it's Deandra because fingerprints don't lie. Please help us through this unexpected event." As I entered the medical examiner's office, I felt God's spirit and his hands guiding and comforting me. It was a presence of God I had never quite felt before. As I looked down at my daughter, I whispered to God "she looks like she is sleeping, so peacefully", and ended my statement to God with "Lord, you even speak in death". In the midst of grief, I turned to God for strength and forgiveness. With faith in my heart, I forgave the man responsible for her death. God's presence was felt deeply and provided me comfort in the midst of immense pain.

All praises be unto God, life has not always been a walk in the park and I can attest that I encountered many stumbling blocks along the way, but Jesus Christ and the Holy Spirit guided me through. God has been before me a light by day and a pillar of fire by night and He is the almighty protector of all the issues of life—period. God's radical love and guidance transformed my life from a state of despair to a newfound sense of peace, love, and righteousness. With His power, I am able to defeat the devil and find relentless joy in my everyday conversations with Him. I am a living testimony of God's grace and mercy. It is the work of the Lord and His love for me that changed a tragedy into a testimony and fills me with a reservoir of wisdom and a cascade of blessings. Today, I am a motivational speaker, dedicated to fighting substance abuse, and the founder of No Limit Recovery. Additionally, I run a successful cleaning company and hold a license as a life and health insurance agent.

Through my many trials and tribulations, I have learned to trust God in all things. He has truly turned my tragedy into triumph, and I am now equipped to inspire others and share the love and faith that have transformed my life.

God has been before me a light by day and a pillar of fire by night and He is the almighty protector of all the issues of life—period.

#NobodyToldMetheRoadWouldBeEasy #ExpressionsofHisGlory

*Mary, Mary; "Can't Give Up Now," SONY BMG Music Entertainment 1999, 2000 Album *Thankful*

Latonya Lucas

Latonya Lucas was raised in Chicago in the Robert Taylor projects known as the Black Belt Community, a segregated community for poor black families. She is the mother of five children: four daughters; Deandra (deceased), Denise, Desiree and Dominique and one son; Devone. In 1991, she dedicated her life to Jesus and began serving in various roles and responsibilities of the church. She earned the title "State Evangelist" and was ordained as a minister specializing in street ministry. Latonya pursued higher education and earned an Associate's Degree in Early Childhood Education. She is a motivational speaker and is the founder of No Limit Recovery, an organization that is dedicated to fighting substance abuse. In addition, her accomplishments include managing a successful cleaning company and being a licensed life and health insurance agent. Her motto is "hold on, my change is coming".

12 | *Evidence of Divine Glory*

The title of this story has an extraordinary and supreme meaning to it, so much so that it is worth taking the time to define.

The word *evidence* can be defined as furnishing proof, the truth of a matter, or a situation. In this case, it's specifically a representative of a written testimony. It bears witness to God's divine glory.

The word *divine* is often biblically described as relating to or coming directly from God.

The word *glory*, in simplest terms, means the manifested presence of the Holy Trinity of GOD—God the Father, God the Son, and the Holy Spirit.

In December of 2010, I said "Yes" to a serious commitment. Just ten months after I received the gift of salvation, the father of my four children proposed to me; if I recall correctly, I gave him a resounding "Yes." We immediately started our wedding planning. Things seemed to be going great, but one day I received a text message from my fiancée that wasn't meant for me but for another woman. I quickly and fiercely confronted him; he stated that she was the wife of a friend—I did not believe him but I didn't cancel the wedding either.

We were married on March 26, 2011, at the Signature Grand; our dream wedding venue. Our wedding was absolutely beautiful, and we were accompanied by the people who loved us the most. However, our honeymoon, for some reason, was unhappy for me. I managed to push through those feelings of unhappiness, and upon arriving home, I discovered that he was still in communication with the young lady.

From that point on, we experienced one issue after another concerning her. So, I did some research and found out that he had been honest about her being married but left out the fact that her husband was incarcerated and had been for a while. This led to our first marital separation for about a year. Eventually, we agreed to give our marriage another chance.

I must admit that we both tried, I even tried to forget about the other lady, but a woman's intuition (a way of feeling or thinking) doesn't cease within her when something is wrong. My intuition had me checking his phone, timing his day, and keeping track of the typical things cheating people do. The information I gathered clearly portrayed that he was in some sort of affair with her.

Discovering this information caused me to become disrespectful towards him. He was seeing a side of Tamika that he had never seen before. The anger and disrespect was as real as could be. Perhaps it came from the years of suspicious repetitive patterns with other women. I had become fed up to the tenth degree with it.

It wasn't long before we separated again. One day he came home from work, the tension between he and I was heavy, but yet SILENT at the same time as I was avoiding arguing with him, so I knelt on the floor and began praying aloud. Before I knew it, my husband stood over me shouting, "You're crazy, and I am done." I didn't move, I kept praying.

When I got up, he was gone. I thought to myself, "He's fire hot (mad), he will cool down and return later." My thought was wrong. Nightfall came, he did not show up. Morning came, he still was not home. Forty eight hours and still there were no signs of him coming back. That's when reality and fear kicked in as I realized change had come between us.

Things progressively hastened between the young lady and him. She began showing up everywhere; at his family's house, at the park (fulfilling a position as a team mom for his football team, the same position I held for over 10 years). As a result, a weight of mental and emotional battles were quickly released over my life.

I felt ashamed, rejected, and disrespected. I blamed myself for our issues as guilt and resentment crept into my life alongside a deeper mental battle of defeat, oppression, and depression.

I tried talking to others about my battle, but whenever I did, he always found out and accused me of making him out to be a faulty man. I now understand how that was a form of manipulation used to confuse me. Confusion surfaced and intensified, my soul craving for him to come back home, but what prevented that from happening was when something else occurred.

One day during football practice, he was rushed to the hospital by paramedics. Everyone at the park thought things were fine between us, so someone informed me of the incident. I made my way over to the emergency room and, to my surprise, his "friend" had driven herself to the hospital in the vehicle that he bought for me as a pre-wedding gift. I felt it was not the time to behave ignorantly, so I got the keys from him and gracefully drove her home and then went back to see if he was okay. I know, I know, I can hear somebody saying "GIRL, you are better than me because I would have handled it differently." You are correctly thinking because the truth of the matter is every person responds to things differently. If you have been through this type of experience, you understand fully what it feels like without me unfolding every single detail. It doesn't feel good, and it most certainly is not for your good.

For me, it triggered thoughts of murder for him (not of a physical murder but nasty and wicked thoughts). It also caused me to have suicidal thoughts (again, not physical death or murder but more so internal thoughts of giving up and not wanting to mortally LIVE). I battled thinking I was crazy or bipolar. I even had thoughts of checking myself into a mental institution. I was so broken, and my internal wounds were bleeding enormously. I remember thinking I can't take another ounce of pain. But one Saturday afternoon, as I dropped off our son to a football game, her presence triggered an emotional reaction for me to behave unseemly. I fought and fought and fought that emotion until I literally fled to my car as a means of pushing back the feelings of rage and anger.

I drove to the beach, sat on a rock, and within two minutes I heard a voice in my head say "Tamika, confess that you hate your husband". I replied quietly, "I don't hate Him" because I was taught that hating someone is not acceptable. Then I heard the voice say "Tamika, confess your faults to one another for I am faithful to forgive them" my response was "but there is no one here with me," then the voice spoke and said "the Father, the Son, and the Holy Spirit is here." Tears started streaming down my face uncontrollably as I hastened to confess that I hated him.

I then felt a presence behind me. At first, I was a little nervous to turn around. Once I looked, I discovered he was a white American man about 25 years of age standing there. He said three words to me *"don't be sad,"* and He walked away. A few moments later he came back to give me a ring (the ring was a pink Disney princess child's ring that normally is purchased from a gumball machine). Then the voice started speaking to me again saying "Tamika, you are my princess, I love you and I want you to learn how to live." I responded by saying I don't know how to *live* life beyond he and I. Tears sprung up and out of my eyes from within the depth of my soul.

I clearly knew that it wasn't just a voice in my head, but God speaking to me. He instructed me to pay attention to everything around me; things like the sky, rocks, sand, and the water. Once I gazed upon the sea waves, God spoke to me saying, "Tamika, the earth is the Lord's and the fullness thereof and all who dwell in it". He continued, "Tamika, Lift up your head because the King of Glory shall come in." I was encouraged by His spoken words, pondered them in my heart, then went home to search the bible to confirm that it was God's voice I was hearing.

I discovered biblical evidence that God was prophetically speaking over my life through His written word (Psalm 24). When God speaks, He moves. From that day forward I saw the King of Glory (God) show up to help me process everything happening in my life. Although letting go took me about ten years, God was with me the entire time. I had legal grounds to divorce him, however the mental and emotional strongholds (soul ties) would not permit me to do so.

Thankfully, I had set healthy boundaries by remaining physically and sexually separated from him for eight years after marriage but unfortunately those unknown internal strings (lust, rejection, depression, low-self-esteem, insecurities, and the list can go on and on) had to be cut and that could only be done by the King of Glory himself (King Jesus).

Now granted, God could have done it quickly, but I believe that the ten years of purging was necessary, It taught me that the old wise saying "when God says 'Yes' nobody can say 'no,'" is only partially the TRUTH, an addition to that Truth is when God says "No" we should never say "Yes." It also revealed that every battle God fights He wins. I couldn't have won the battle by myself. There's a song by Yolanda Adams titled "The battle is not yours, it's the Lord's." Yes, indeed for me it was the Lord's Battle. Now don't get me wrong there was times I had to fight with weapons of prayer, praise, and worship (praising God in dance freed me from a lot of mental strongholds and helped transform my love for a man towards the love for GOD).

Just as God's deliverance was manifesting in my life my husband contacted me and asked if I wanted our marriage or not. I had a rush of emotions. "Is this of God or of the enemy?" I pondered. You would think that my answer would have been "No" right away but it wasn't. It was, "Let me get back to you." A couple days later I called him with some questions, I wanted to see where his heart and mind truly were. That did not turn out well and within two months I understood why. A situation (out of moral respect I'd rather not disclose the sensitive nature) occurred in his life that required my children and I to support him. To my surprise the same lady showed up there too. This almost took me right back to the original place of battling in pain, I literally felt every mental and emotional battle all over again. It was a frightening feeling.

Upon arriving home I prayed and went to bed. While asleep I had a symbolic dream. In the dream there was this longgggggggggggg string in my belly. I begin to pull it out through my mouth and it seemed to be never ending, but finally I came to the end of it and I cut it. Then I jumped up out of my sleep and God said to me "The soul tie has been cut." Listen, it's hard to contain my praise right here. I've got a praise that unless you been through this type of soul-tie you wouldn't understand it—so I'll just say *"thank you, Jesus!"*

The next week, I filed for a divorce which settled in court on

May 11, 2022. Since then, I have been on a continual healing process with God. I can't say that my wounds did not create scars and that my scars don't try to make me feel useless or unworthy at times, but the one thing I stand on is the fact that I have *Evidence of His Divine Glory*—The King of Glory came in to my life and wiped every tear. He fought every battle. He is the reason I am still here.

Praise Break - GLORYYYYYYYYYYYYYYY! Hallelujah! Thank you King of Glory "JESUS" for fighting my every battle to set me free!

In closing, I'll say only 1/4 of my story was shared in this message beloved ones of GOD. I can't tell it all at one time. So I'll leave you with this. You don't know! "You just don't know what all I've been through, all the mental and emotional things God brought me through, all the tears I've cried, all the things I kept bottled up inside, all the many times that I prayed over and over again but things didn't change." These words by *Zacardi Cortez, tell my story. You don't know all that I endured to gain the prophetic moment and opportunity to proclaim "Evidence of God's Divine Glory" story to you.

God's glory has been real in my life and can be real in your life. As a matter of fact, I decree and I declare Psalm 24 over your life, in Jesus' name and I pray my story was uplifting and encouraging to you. More of my testimony is written in my first book titled, *Finally Free to Be Me: Whom the Son Sets Free is Free Indeed!*

To God be all the Glory!

The King of Glory came in to my life and wiped every tear. He fought every battle. He is the reason I am still here.

#EvidenceofDivineGlory #ExpressionsofHisGlory

---

*Cortez, Zacardi; "You Just Don't Know," Black Smoke Music Worldwide 2019, Album *Imprint* 2022

Tamika Baldwin

Tamika is the mother of 4 adult children (3 Favored Young Men & 1 Fearfully & Wonderfully made Daughter.) The grandmother of 10 Double Blessed grandchildren;more importantly she is a born again believer by the grace of Jesus Christ. Her rebirth encounter occurred on January 31, 2010 under the Leadership of Pastor George and First Lady Jestina Bowles at Bread of Life Christian Center. After starting her new life in Christ, she went back to school in 2013 and successfully earned her High School Diploma at Atlantic Technical Trade School. She utilized her learned skills as a Home Health Aide to serve and care for her grandmother; until she transitioned into Heaven (July 25,2022). She Graduated in 2020 from Daughter's of Zion Mentorship Program and was elected most congenial mentee. She is the published author of *Free to Be Me: Whom the Son Sets Free is Free Indeed* (her personal memoir) and *Finally Free A-Z Prayer Journal*. Her favorite scripture is 1st Peter 2:9 But ye are a chosen generation, a royal priesthood, an holy nation, a peculiar people; that ye should show forth the praises of him who hath called you out of darkness into his marvelous light.

YOU WRITE, WE PUBLISH, TOGETHER WE CREATE

DIVINE WORKS PUBLISHING, LLC.

A co-publishing service for indie authors seeking a strategic bigger partner alliance for greater visibility and success in today's marketplace.

www.DivineWorksPublishing.com

561-990-BOOK (2665)

info@ DivineWorksPublishing.com

www.ingramcontent.com/pod-product-compliance
Lightning Source LLC
Chambersburg PA
CBHW030200100526
44592CB00009B/375